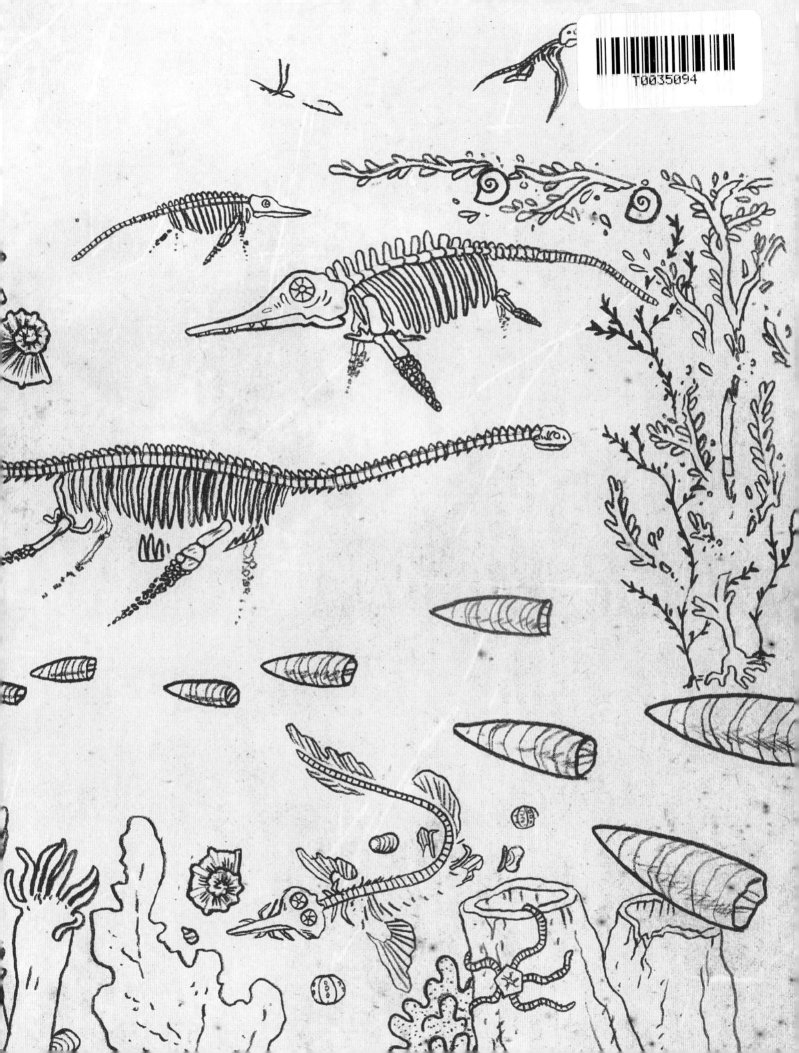

For Papa, who tells
the best stories —S. G. M.

For Amelia and Eliza:
Stay curious —M. W.

Published by Roaring Brook Press
Roaring Brook Press is a division of
Holtzbrinck Publishing Holdings Limited Partnership
120 Broadway, New York, NY 10271 • mackids.com

Library of Congress Control Number: 2021906559
ISBN 978-1-250-14021-0

Our books may be purchased in bulk for promotional,
educational, or business use. Please contact your local
bookseller or the Macmillan Corporate and Premium
Sales Department at (800) 221-7945 ext. 5442 or by email at
MacmillanSpecialMarkets@macmillan.com.

First edition, 2021 • Book design by Sharismar Rodriguez
The illustrations for this book were created with HB pencil on
plain printer paper, scanned, and colored in Photoshop.
Printed in China by RR Donnelley Asia Printing Solutions Ltd.,
Dongguan City, Guangdong Province

10 9 8 7 6 5 4 3 2 1

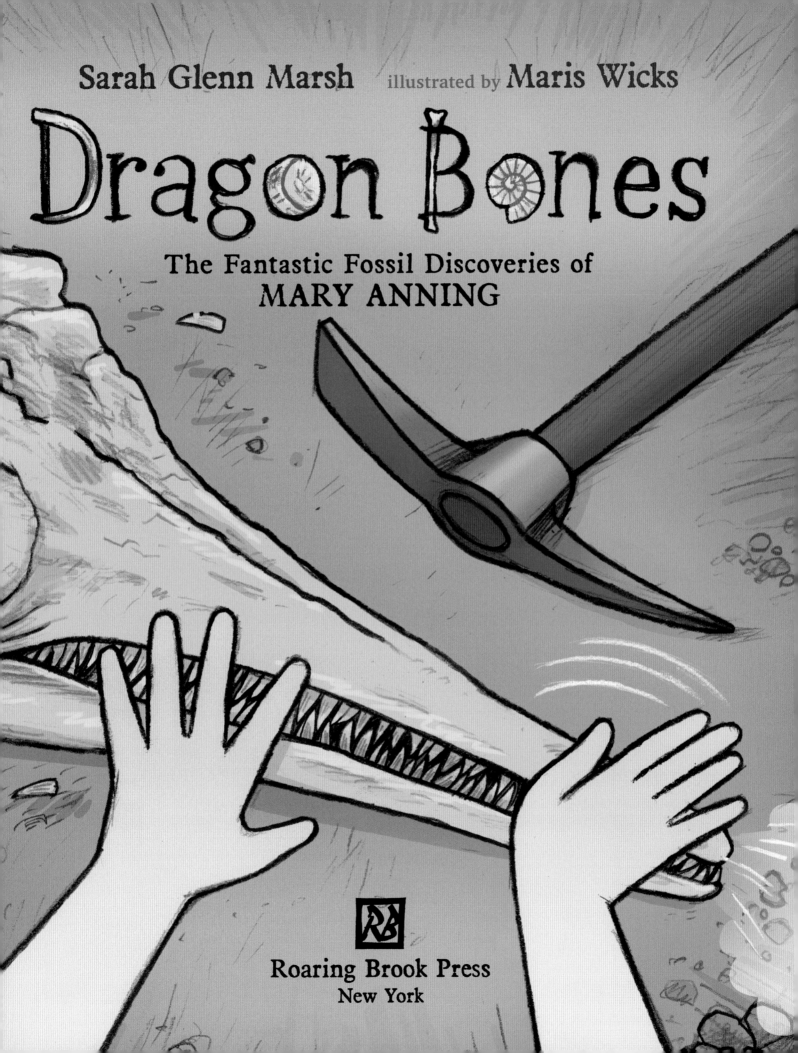

Sarah Glenn Marsh   illustrated by Maris Wicks

Dragon Bones

The Fantastic Fossil Discoveries of MARY ANNING

Roaring Brook Press
New York

Little Mary Anning loved to treasure hunt.

Her home in the seaside town of Lyme Regis, England,
was often chilly and damp from storms that rolled in off the sea.

Sometimes the storms would even flood the Annings' house, bringing the sea indoors and forcing them out.

But Mary loved the storms, because when rain pounded the cliffs, it washed away mud and uncovered new, unusual things from deep within the rocky earth.

And that meant
treasure-hunting time.

Under rubble, through puddles,
inside tunnels, and with her trusty tools,
Mary searched for buried treasures.

Mary always wanted to be the first to spot something more than an ordinary rock poking out of the mud.

After their treasure hunts, the Anning family sold their finds to tourists.

They called the fossilized shells and bones "curios," short for "curiosities."

Mary hated to sell the curios. She longed to slip a few treasures into her pocket to study alone later. She knew they contained forgotten stories and hidden secrets.

But there were food shortages all over England, and her family needed money to eat.

So Mary sold . . .

snakestones,

devil's fingers,

and verteberries

. . . wondering all the
while what secrets they held.

The Anning family was a great treasure-hunting team.

Until one day, when Mary's father,
who had been sick for some time,
passed away after a fall.

Now Mary had to lead the treasure hunts, scaling the high cliffs while her spirits sank low. Under rubble, through puddles, inside tunnels, and with her trusty tools, Mary searched for buried treasures and imagined her father digging beside her.

In the winter,
wind, rain, and snow
made dangerous
landslides common.

But wild weather revealed the
most treasures, so even in harsh
conditions, they hunted.

As she worked, Mary imagined digging up something no one had ever seen. There was no telling what stories the hard-packed earth might be hiding. No telling what secrets her shovel would strike next.

Shipwrecked gold?

A necklace of precious gemstones?
A bone from a whale that ate ships?
MARY!

Her brother, Joseph, had discovered
something no one had ever seen.

He thought it was a giant crocodile head.
What a treasure! Mary worked hard to find
the rest of the creature.

Joseph soon gave up, but Mary kept searching. The hope of discovery made her return to the cliffs again and again, even when she had to go alone.

TNK
TNK
TNK
TNK

When she finally found it, she pictured her father's proud face as she stood beside the bones. That was better than any treasure.

The giant crocodile skeleton made headlines in the newspapers. It was a fine example of a fossil, the remains of a plant or animal that have turned to stone over time—just like Mary's other treasures.

A fossil collector bought the skeleton from Mary, and the creature was displayed at a museum, where someone named it "ichthyosaur." That meant "fish lizard."

ICHTHYOSAUR

It looked more like a dragon to Mary.

After that, Mary dreamed of strange, nameless creatures curled in the cliffs.

Beasts with claws and sharp teeth . . .

beasts with scales and rustling wings . . .

beasts with fins and long necks . . .

. . . all waiting for her to discover them.

Years passed. Mary found several more ichthyosaur fossils. To understand how they fit together, she dissected fish and studied their skeletons.

Under rubble, through puddles, inside tunnels, and with her trusty tools, Mary searched for buried treasures and took them home to study like she'd always wanted.

She missed having Joseph on her hunts, but her new friend Tray was great at sniffing out treasure.

One winter, Mary discovered something unlike any fossil she had found before.

Through wind and rain,
she carefully unearthed the
mysterious creature that would
become her next major discovery.

A man bought the skeleton and named
it "plesiosaur," which meant "near-lizard."
He wrote papers about it that lots of scientists
read with amazement. He never mentioned Mary.

But she kept hunting.

When she was twenty-seven years old, Mary opened
Anning's Fossil Depot, a shop where she could display
the fossils she found and show the world the secrets
they held.

But still, what Mary
Anning loved best of all was
treasure hunting. Whenever a storm
rolled in off the sea, tourists and townspeople
would find Anning's Fossil Depot closed
for the day.

After all . . .

. . . there was always
another treasure waiting
to be discovered.

MORE ABOUT MARY

Mary Anning (1799–1847) was considered the mother of paleontology before the discipline even had a name. But she was also something of a legend in her small English town of Lyme Regis from the time she was born. When she was a toddler, she was struck by lightning while playing with a neighbor in the snow. Remarkably, Mary survived what should have killed her. She became part of the local lore—many credited her intelligence and lively personality to the lightning strike, as though these traits were supernatural gifts. However, for most of her life, Mary wasn't recognized for her many contributions to science; wealthy men bought her fossils and took credit for her work when displaying them in museums. This pained Mary, who had as much or more hands-on experience with fossils than her male contemporaries.

When she was 13, she found her first skeleton dating from the time of the dinosaurs: an ichthyosaur. Her brother had unearthed the creature's head several months prior. This discovery fueled her strong curiosity, and soon she discovered the first complete *Plesiosaurus*, followed by a pterosaur known as the *Dimorphodon macronyx*, a *Squaloraja* fish skeleton, and another type of plesiosaur, the *Plesiosaurus macrocephalus*. Mary began dissecting fish to better understand the anatomy of her discoveries and learned how to draw the creatures she found. She was becoming a scientist, making observations about her treasures and building on the research of others. From 1826 on, Mary met with European and American geologists and fossil collectors at her own store, Anning's Fossil Depot.

Mary soon began working and corresponding with other scientists such as Scottish geologist Charles Lyell and English geologist and priest Adam Sedgwick. When she discovered the first pterosaur skeleton outside Germany (the *Dimorphodon macronyx*), William Buckland, an English theologian and geologist, credited Mary with finding the fossil when he presented his observations on it to the Geological Society of London. She also worked with Swiss naturalist Louis Agassiz during his visit to her hometown in 1834. She so impressed him that in 1837 he named the fossil fish *Acrodus anningiae* after her, the only person to name a species for her in her lifetime. Mary's fossils also inspired geologist Henry De la Beche's renowned 1830 watercolor painting *Duria Antiquior*, which helped people begin to understand life as it existed in the past, paving the way for more groundbreaking discoveries.

MARY'S DRAGONS:

Meet the Ichthyosaur

This was Mary's first major discovery. After her brother, Joseph, found the ichthyosaur's head in 1811, Mary unearthed the rest of its body in November 1812. This was not the first ichthyosaur fossil ever discovered, but it brought the Anning family to the attention of Britain's scientific community.

QUICK FACTS:
- Early Triassic to late Cretaceous: They first appeared about 250 million years ago, and at least one species of ichthyosaur survived until 94 million years ago.
- Nickname: Fish Lizard
- Water dweller (marine reptile).
- Different species varied from 3 to 60 feet in length.
- They were carnivores, with a large variety of prey in the ocean, because different species adapted to eat different things over millions of years.
- Some species were top aquatic predators in their time.

- Like today's dolphins and whales, ichthyosaurs breathed air.
- They bore live young in the water.
- Bite marks on fossils suggest they may have bitten one another's snouts during conflicts.

Meet the *Plesiosaurus dolichodeirus*

In December 1823, Mary discovered a complete skeleton of a *Plesiosaurus dolichodeirus*. This finding was significant because this creature more closely resembled modern reptiles than the ichthyosaur. When geologist William Conybeare lectured about this find at the Geological Society of London, he failed to mention her name even once.

QUICK FACTS:
- Early Jurassic: They first appeared about 197 million years ago and survived until about 190 million years ago.
- Nickname: Near-Lizard
- Water dweller (marine reptile).
- Distinctly shaped, this early plesiosaur had a small head, long neck, and large body with flippers and a short tail. It flapped all four flippers to propel itself through the water.
- Grew to about 15 feet in length.

- Early plesiosaurs ate fish and belemnites, the ancestors of squids.
- Like today's whales and dolphins, they gave birth to live young in the water.

Meet the *Dimorphodon macronyx*

In December 1828, Mary discovered the first pterosaur skeleton ever found outside Germany. When William Buckland presented his paper on the fossil, it was one of the rare occasions on which Mary was actually credited with the discovery.

QUICK FACTS:
- Early Jurassic: They first appeared around 202 million years ago and survived until about 197 million years ago.
- Land dweller capable of flight (reptile).
- This early pterosaur had a large head and eyes, a heavy body, and a wingspan of about 5 feet. The long tail probably stabilized its flight.
- *Dimorphodon*'s sturdy legs and relatively short wingspan for its weight may indicate that it took to the air infrequently, perhaps as a last resort when threatened.
- Highly developed hands and feet suggest this creature could climb well, like a squirrel.
- Fossils have mainly been found in coastal regions.
- Tooth analysis shows *Dimorphodon* probably ate insects and small land vertebrates.
- Pterosaurs laid soft-shelled eggs, like snakes and lizards.

Meet the *Dapedium politum*

Mary found this ancient ray-finned fish in November 1828. The skeleton was in such perfect condition that one newspaper called it "unrivaled."

QUICK FACTS:
- Early Jurassic: They first appeared about 197 million years ago and survived until about 190 million years ago.
- Water dweller (bony fish).

- About 13 inches in length.
- It had a flat but deep body, like a dinner plate.
- Although it had a small mouth, its powerful jaws and blunt teeth allowed it to crush hard-shelled invertebrates such as mussels and sea urchins.
- They were the favorite fish dinner of ichthyosaurs.

Meet the *Squaloraja polyspondyla*

Discovered by Mary in December 1829, the skeleton of this ancient fish attracted attention because it had certain traits of modern sharks and rays.

QUICK FACTS:
- Early Jurassic: They first appeared about 197 million years ago and survived until about 191 million years ago.
- Water dweller (cartilaginous fish).
- A bottom-feeder, it inhabited shallow marine areas.
- It had a skeleton made of cartilage, not bone, like sharks and rays.
- Had a long tail, though the skeleton Mary found was missing its tail.

Meet the *Plesiosaurus macrocephalus*

In December 1830, Mary discovered another nearly complete plesiosaur skeleton, this time a different species called *Plesiosaurus macrocephalus*. When Richard Owen presented his analysis of the specimen in 1839, he failed to mention Mary, referencing only the man who had purchased the fossil and made it available for his study.

QUICK FACTS:
- Early Jurassic: They first appeared about 197 million years ago and survived until about 190 million years ago.
- Water dweller (marine reptile).
- This early plesiosaur had a bigger head with fewer and thicker neck bones than *Plesiosaurus dolichodeirus*. (*Macrocephalus* means "big head.")
- This plesiosaurs inhabited oceans worldwide.
- They bore live young in the water.
- It is theorized that they ate everything from bony fish to hard- and soft-bodied cephalopods.
- Fossils from this species of plesiosaur show evidence of bone death, suggesting that like humans, they could get the bends, or decompression sickness, after deep ocean dives.

HOW TO BECOME A PALEONTOLOGIST

Do you love spending time outdoors? Digging in the dirt for hidden treasures? Do you want to make amazing discoveries that contribute to our understanding of the past? Do you love learning about dinosaurs, or even about the history of life on earth? Then you may want to become a paleontologist, just like Mary! Read on for some ways you can get started in this exciting field.

WHAT EXACTLY DOES A PALEONTOLOGIST DO?

Field paleontologists study geological maps and plan prospecting trips to look for fossils of plants and animals. When they find a fossil, they document its location and position in the rock formation with detailed notes, as Mary once did. Then they carefully remove the fossils and take them where they can be cleaned, studied, and preserved. In the lab, paleontologists examine the fossils, describing them in minute detail and comparing them to others, and write about their findings so everyone can learn more about the earth's past.

A paleontologist might work at a college or university, at a museum, or for the government. They each focus on one of several different branches of paleontology—including, of course, dinosaurs!

WHAT SHOULD YOU STUDY TO BECOME A PALEONTOLOGIST?

Being a paleontologist requires a lot of time in school; you will need a PhD, or doctorate degree, to work in this field—the highest degree offered by universities! In other words, if this is something you want to do, you'll need to be as passionate as Mary about spending a lot of time reading and studying.

TO GET A TASTE FOR LIFE AS A PALEONTOLOGIST:

- Attend a summer camp focused on natural sciences.
- Take as many math and science classes as possible, and develop your reading comprehension and computer skills.
- Visit museums with fossil displays, such as the Smithsonian National Museum of Natural History. If there are no museums near you, view fossils online with a responsible adult at sites such as fossilmuseum.net.
- Volunteer with a nearby museum or college to work with fossils yourself.

SERIOUS ABOUT BEING A PALEONTOLOGIST?

· In college, choose a biology or geology major, or both.

· Complete internships that give you experience in the field.

· Study and work a few more years in graduate school
to get your PhD in paleontology!

SELECTED BIBLIOGRAPHY

Blocks Rock. "STEM Career Inspiration for Kids: Paleontologists."
blocksrock.com/news-and-research/stem-career-inspiration-for
-kids-paleontologists.

Cadbury, Deborah. *The Dinosaur Hunters: A True Story of Scientific Rivalry and the
Discovery of the Prehistoric World.* London: Fourth Estate, 2000.

Davis, Larry E. "Mary Anning: Princess of Palaeontology and Geological Lioness." *Compass: Earth Science Journal
of Sigma Gamma Epsilon* 84, no. 1 (2012): 57–88.

Dorey, Fran. "A Timeline of Fossil Discoveries." Australian Museum. Updated December 23, 2019. australian
.museum/learn/science/human-evolution/a-timeline-of-fossil-discoveries/.

Emling, Shelley. *The Fossil Hunter: Dinosaurs, Evolution, and the Woman Whose Discoveries Changed the World.*
New York: Palgrave Macmillan, 2009.

EnvironmentalScience.org. "What Is a Paleontologist?" environmentalscience.org/career/paleontologist.

Garwood, Russell. "Life as a Palaeontologist: Palaeontology for Dummies, Part 2." Palaeontology Online. 2014.
palaeontologyonline.com/articles/2014/life-as-a-palaeontologist-palaeontology-for-dummies-part-2/.

Goodhue, Thomas W. "Mary Anning: The Fossilist as Exegete." *Endeavour* 29, no. 1 (March 2005): 28–32.

McGowan, Christopher. *The Dragon Seekers.* Cambridge, MA: Perseus Publishing, 2001.

Torrens, Hugh. "Mary Anning (1799–1847) of Lyme; 'The Greatest Fossilist the World Ever Knew.'"
British Journal for the History of Science 25, no. 3 (September 1995): 257–84.

University of California Museum of Paleontology. "Mary Anning (1799–1847)."
ucmp.berkeley.edu/history/anning.html.